"The magic begins when a herd of elephants walks silently past my jeep. It's a welcome sight on my way to camp."

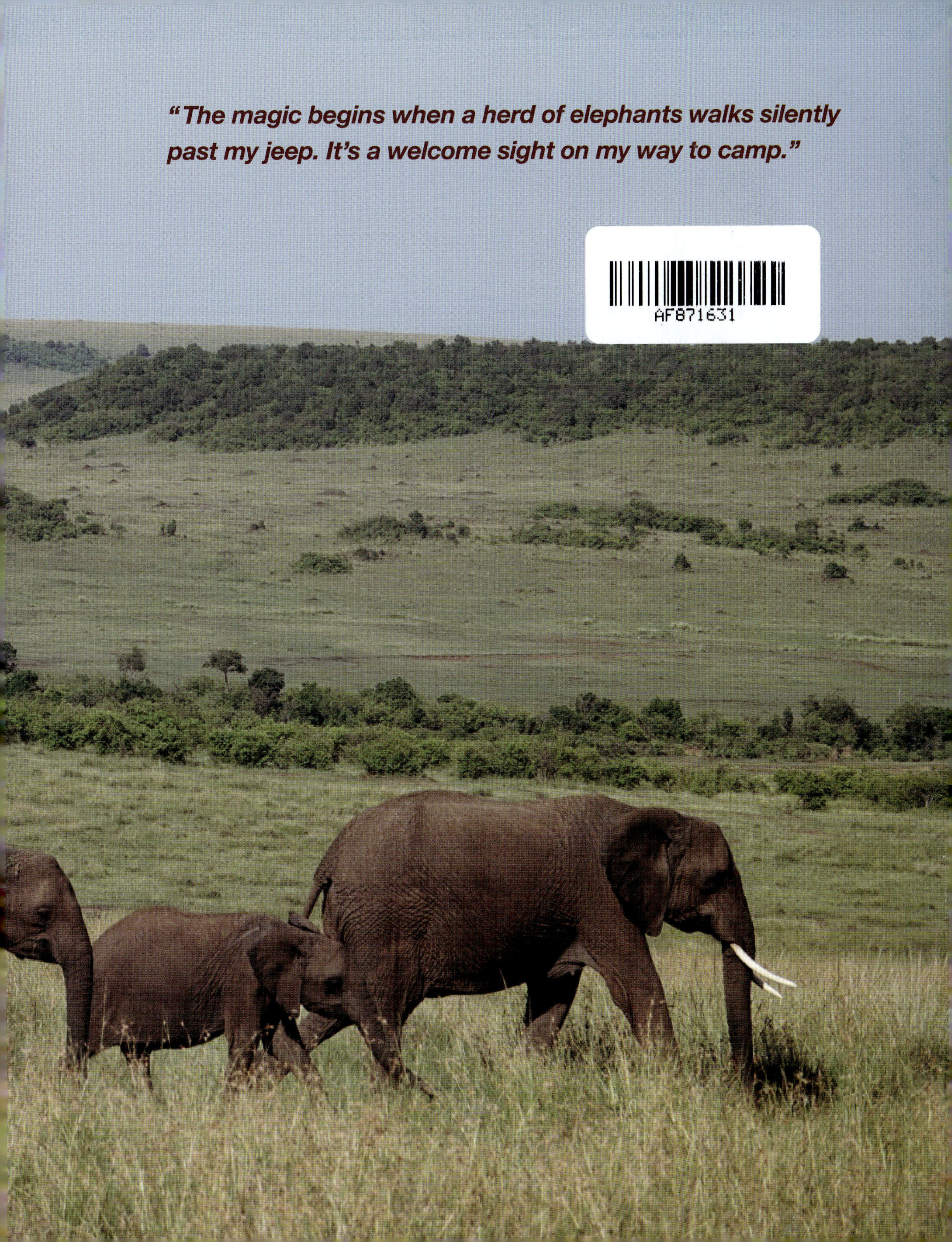

ADVENTURES IN THE *wild* WITH JAN LATTA

TRUE TO LIFE BOOKS

Educating children about endangered animals.
Jan Latta author and wildlife photographer.

CONTENTS

WILD AFRICA

"The first time a lion walked up to my jeep, I was nervous. My guide told me not to be frightened, as lions only identify with the smell of the jeep."

Up close and sometimes scary.

This is my eleventh trip to Africa. I'm so glad the 26-hour flight is over and Nairobi is now safe after another bomb scare. I say hello to the wonderful staff at Macushla House and fall into bed. Early the next morning after a manic taxi ride to Wilson airport, I climb into the 12-seater plane for a bumpy ride to the Mara. I like flying in small planes because they fly low and I have a bird's-eye view of the landscape.

The Rekero camp guide is waiting for me on the dirt landing strip. Hurray, now my safari (a Swahili word for journey) adventure begins.

It's my fourth time at Rekero camp and it's great to see my tent again. I quickly unpack and say hello to

Traditional clothes are proudly worn by the staff.

My jeep is open on all sides, for photography.

Three cheetah brothers after the morning hunt.

The jeep provides a shady rest for a leopard.

Stacey, the camp manager. I eat a healthy lunch, then greet my Maasai guide, Nic. I jump into the jeep and off we go! Nic wears a red shuka to keep warm and he brings an extra one for me because it's very cold in the afternoon, especially in the open jeep.

I've researched all the animals I might see on this trip, so it's exciting when a wild animal allows the jeep to come close to it. I'm less than two metres from a male lion and for half an hour, I photograph his funny, goofy expressions – he's posing for me and showing off, just like a domestic house cat.

During the night the ranger will carry a runga stick and bang it on the ground when a hippo is close to my tent. I don't mind the munch, munch sounds of nibbled grass, or their soft contented musical notes, but when they fight each other in the river, it's an angry grunting and honking sound. They also have a loud fart and a nasty habit of swishing dung into the next hippo's face. Yuk!

Hippos are the most dangerous animals in Africa. If I get between them and the river they will attack me because they are fiercely territorial. Surprisingly, on their tiny hooves, they can run faster than me, so I never walk close to the river without my guide.

FUN FLYING !

I love flying in Africa – from the tiny six-seater Cessna, to the big commercial planes. I have my nose pressed to the window to see herds of animals – elephants, thousands of wildebeest and the long shadows left behind after a journey of giraffes.

When the pilot is ready to land, he circles the dirt runway to check if any wild animals are on the landing strip, and then comes the bumpy, dusty landing.

"It was a great thrill to see leopards in the wild at Rekero Camp."

Bella 2, the beautiful blue-eyed leopard.

There's a noise outside my tent I can't identify – it's the rustle of leaves followed by munching sounds. I hold my breath and listen. Then I hear the deep stomach rumble of a large animal. I open the flap of my tent and I'm amazed to see a magnificent bull elephant, a big tusker, just a metre away. I watch him eating, and as I'm not in any danger, I go back to bed.

Did I dream about an elephant outside my tent? No, I didn't because there's a big dollop of wet dung plopped just outside. Elephants' dung is called the 'fertilizer' in Africa, but it's a bit pongy so near to my tent. I wiggle my torchlight into the sky and that's the sign for the ranger to walk me to the jeep. It's dark, very cold and dangerous.

I've come to Rekero Camp to see the elusive leopards. My guide Nic finds Bahati and her daughter, Bella 2, who is famous for her blue eyes. But you'll have to wait until the leopard chapter on page 30 to read about it. Oh, can you wait that long?

My adventure continues when Nic stops in front of a lioness resting in the bush. She looks at me and keeps eye contact with me as she walks towards the jeep. I'm thrilled and a bit frightened. She is right next to the jeep, still looking up at me. Then she turns, walks around and disappears into the bush. Nic says, "You didn't take a photo?" and I reply, "No, it was so special to have such direct eye-contact with a wild lioness."

Water buck posing perfectly.

The magestic male impala.

The shy elan.

One morning I complain to Nic about a terrible smell. He laughs and tells me that a herd of buffalo walked past about half an hour before. Phew, their awful pong stays around for a long time.

On the way back to camp we stop to see my favourite animal, the cheetah. She is resting in the grass with her three young cubs. We don't want to disturb her so we leave, but I do hope I see her again.

In the afternoon a cranky rhino is terrorizing the tourists. Ten minutes later he is thundering out of the bush, with dust and dirt flying everywhere, just behind our jeep. I yelp a loud warning, but the rhino gets closer and closer to our jeep. We finally pick up speed and escape from him. Wow, that was scary! Rhinos have very poor eyesight and they charge at anything that moves. A jeep seems to be one of their favourite targets.

After dinner I discover a hot water bottle tucked into my bed and in the morning there's another one in the jeep for me. What a luxury! I will be snug and warm all the way to my next stop, which is the Encounter Mara camp.

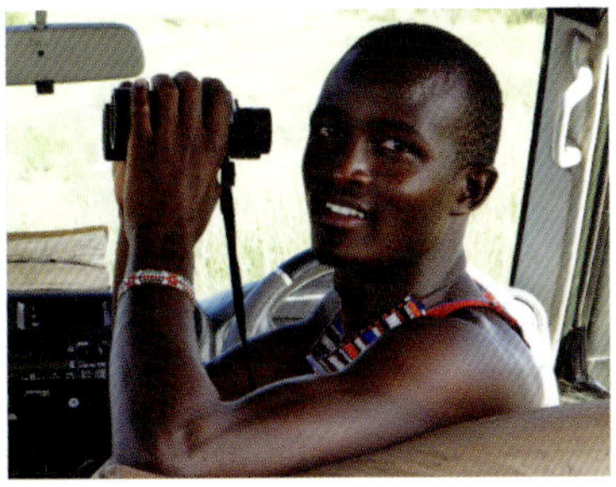

My guide is very knowledgeable about all the animals.

THE TOOTHBRUSH TREE

The Maasai people clean their teeth using twigs from the pepper tree. The outer layer is scraped away and splayed out to make the bristles of a toothbrush. It was so clever, I had to try it! My guide said they don't go to the chemist because there are so many plants containing natural medicines in the bush.

The Big Five – lion, elephant, leopard, buffalo and rhino.

"Searching for the Big Five at Encounter Mara Camp is a challenge."

Encounter Mara Camp is a special place for me because the Mara Naboisho Conservancy only allows a few camps in the area and there's a restriction on the number of jeeps that can be close to a wild animal. I hope I see the Big Five this week.

On the first morning I hear hyenas snarling and growling as they try to steal a lion's kill. My new guide, called Francis, tells me the lion will have to give up his kill because he can't compete with the vicious scavengers. The lion slinks away and the pride will go hungry today.

I go back to camp for lunch and a shower. Francis calls the camp when we are close and a bucket of hot water is waiting for me. The bucket is tipped into my shower unit with the help of a rope outside. I love a bush shower! After I wash my socks and put them on the tent rope I remember I must guard them because thieving baboons stole them once before. What did they do with them? It's funny to imagine them prancing around wearing my socks!

A lioness gathering up her cubs before hunting.

In the afternoon the lion drama continues with a lioness and her three cubs. She picks each cub up in her mouth and hides them under a bush. She is ready to hunt now, and starts to stalk a zebra. The guinea fowls screech a loud warning and the zebra is very nervous, looking around for the predator. Francis drives away because he doesn't want to interfere with the hunt. The lioness fails, but we see her the next morning with a full

tummy, so that's good. The little cubs are so cute. They waddle as they walk after feeding.

During the day I see the comical warthogs, a mongoose family scurrying across the savannah, a cheetah with her kill, and thousands of buffalo, but there are no rhinos left in the area. It's so sad because they are still being killed for their horns. Their horns are made of keratin, the same material as our fingernails, but it is just awful to kill a rhino for that.

The bonus of the day is a leopard hiding in a bush. Two jeeps wait for her to come out, but when she doesn't, the jeeps leave. We decide to wait, and half an hour later the leopard leaves her hiding place and walks towards me. What a reward for our patience!

On the way back to camp there is a glorious sunset as a lonely elephant lumbers across the horizon. A perfect way to end the day.

Warthogs always kneel down to eat because their necks are too short to reach the grass.

Time for a snooze.

A PRIDE OF LIONS

How to get close to a lion without being eaten.

It's 7.00pm at Nabiosho Camp. I'm in the mess tent having dinner with Roelof, the camp manager, when there is a loud bang and the sound of crashing hooves. To my horror a lion is chasing a wildebeest right through the middle of our tent. I'm terrified and don't know what to do, so I stand very still. The lion kills the wildebeest near the staff quarters, but the rest of the pride is prowling around the camp. What should I do? Can I get back to my tent? I'm so frightened.

Roelof suggests two Maasai men walk me to my tent. Now, I'm rigid with fear and try to be as invisible as possible between the men. They swing their torches around and I see some of the pride lurking in the grass. But, just beyond my tent there is a lion with its eyes glowing in the torchlight. I say, "There's a lion just beyond my tent, it's too dangerous to keep walking!" They reply, "It is okay Jan, because you are closer to your tent than the lion is." Aaahhh!!! The desire to run is intense, but I know I must trust my guides, they are so knowledgeable about the lion's behaviour. I walk nervously with them until I'm safe inside my tent.

The pride surrounds the camp every night, and when they roar the sound vibrates through my body. The next morning I hear the pant-breath of a lion right next to my tent. It's so close, but I'm safe.

Each day we check a lioness, her two cubs and a wildebeest kill. On my last day at the camp we check if she still has her kill safely hidden in the bush.

"I love watching mothers with their cubs; they are so affectionate and protective."

On the way we see a huge male lion walking towards her area. This is very dangerous because the male will demand the wildebeest remains, or he might kill the cubs to mate with the lioness. My guide stops and we wait. The big male starts to plod down the hill towards the lioness. She is tense, and snarls at the male. What is going to happen?

The cubs are nervous, but one starts to crawl on its tummy, stalking the male. What is he doing? This is so dangerous for the cub. He gets closer and closer and I hold my breath. The lion whacks the cub on the head, then plonk, falls asleep on the grass. It is daddy, so the family is safe.

The next night was filled with the throaty sounds of lions roaring. In the morning my guide discovers the reason – a pride of lions made a kill during the night. I jump into the jeep and we find the pride. I watch as the male demands to eat first, then the females and the cubs last. Terrible fights break out during the feeding frenzy, then with full tummies, peace is restored.

Fights break out during the feeding frenzy.

What is a pug mark ?

It's the imprint of a lion's paw in the dirt.

Lions always greet each other by rubbing heads together.

"This big male lion walked up to my jeep and flopped down on the grass. It was fun to take photographs of his expressions from a wiggly-tongue yawn, to funny goofy looks."

The lion is trying to hide his kill in a safe place behind a tree.

"Nothing is left to waste in Africa. After the lion has eaten, the hyenas, jackals and vultures wait their turn to devour the leftovers."

The jackals are fearless and try to steal some of the food.

The vultures patiently wait for the lion to finish eating.

The hyenas take over the carcass and fan their tails with excitement. Terrible squabbles and fights break out amongst the clan and the noise is deafening.

GENTLE GIANTS

"An elephant's trunk is very special and it's used for everything ... eating, drinking, friendly fights, having a shower and saying hello."

I always enjoy it when a herd of elephants surrounds my jeep. It's entertaining watching the tiny calves swirling their rubbery trunks around and around. They don't seem to know what to do with the strange, wobbly attachments on their heads. Their mothers will teach them how to suck up water and how to feed with their little trunks. Baby elephants often steal grass from their mothers' mouths, until they get used to feeding themselves. Young female elephants are called 'aunties' and they stay close to the babies especially when a predator is near. The aunties form a protective circle around the young calves who are safe in the centre.

My guide warns me that male elephants are dangerous during the mating season. When a big bull in 'musth' charges the jeep, I'm terrified, but it's a mock charge and the elephant stops in a cloud of dust, just before the jeep. If a mother elephant charges the jeep to protect her tiny calf, I put my fear aside because that is natural, and it's always a mock charge.

The matriach, the oldest female elephant, is very wise and has an imprint in her brain to guide the herd to fresh grass and water. We drive to the river to wait for the herd to arrive.

Aunties always protect a young calf from danger.

After half an hour I hear the soft rumbling and loud trumpeting of the elephants arriving, because it's a social event when herds meet at the river. The young calves squeal with delight as they play in the water, they squirt each other and roll in the mud. But getting up the muddy river bank is a challenge so their mothers come to the rescue by putting their huge trunks under the babies to help them.

Elephants can swim underwater, so if the river is deep enough, they plunge into the water and use their trunks as a snorkel. I love watching this. When they are squeaky clean, they have a lovely roll in the mud again and then toss dust and dirt all over their bodies. Now they are dirty again, but this will protect their skin from biting insects and it will also protect the babies from being sunburnt.

Elephants are very intelligent and it's wonderful to watch these gentle giants communicate with each other. There is so much we need to learn about their emotions and their ability to communicate over great distances. Elephants are still being killed for their ivory tusks. Governments all over the world are trying to stop the terrible slaughter of these family-loving gentle giants. We should all try and help to save the endangered elephants in the world.

Elephants dig in the ground to find water. Grass and small shrubs are dug up with the elephant's foot and trunk.

Elephants wrap their trunks around each other as a sign of affection o

DID YOU KNOW ?

The African elephant's ear is the shape of the map of Africa!

The matriach leading the herd to the river. The big bulls can drink up to 212 litres of water in five minutes.

excitement. But when the trunk is raised, it could be a threat to fight.

A baby greedily slurps its milk from an oversized baby's milk bottle. It took many years to perfect the milk formula.

"I adopted a tiny baby elephant called Mbegu at the Sheldrick Orphanage.

She had spear wounds in her little body and she touched my heart.

Mbegu survived with the care of her keepers. Now she is the mini-matriach of the new nursery babies."

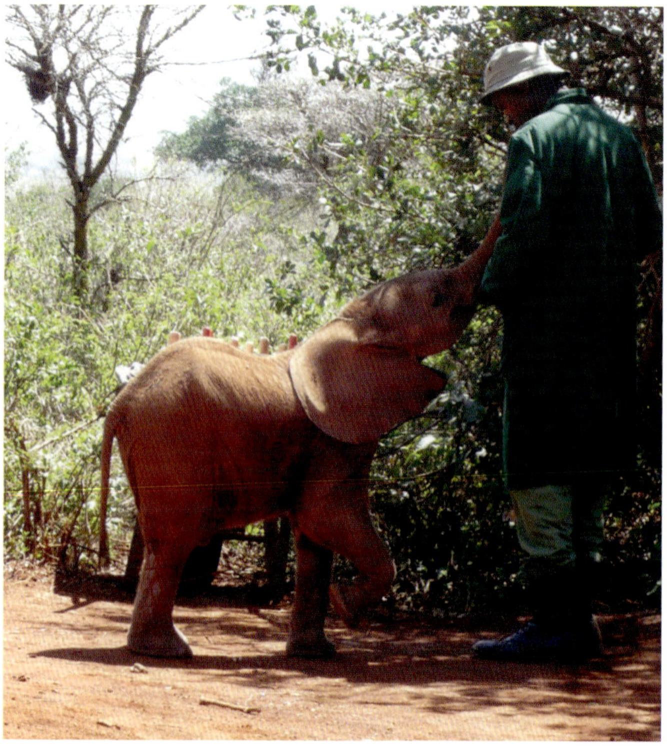

There is a very special bond between the keepers and the young orphans.

Four years ago a tiny baby elephant was rescued from angry villagers by the Sheldrick staff. They gently wrapped her in blankets and comforted her during the flight to Nairobi. She was taken to the nursery and given the name, Mbegu, which means 'tiny seed' in Swahili. She was only seven-weeks old. Her wounds were cleaned with green clay, and she healed quickly.

She developed a loving, caring personality and always protects the new nursery babies. One baby follows Mbegu around so she can suck on her ears, because it comforts her. Isn't that so sweet!

At the Sheldrick centre there is a rhino called Maxwell. When Mbegu and her naughty orphans want to steal some of his lucerne pellets, he sprays the area with pee. Squealing with displeasure, the orphans make a quick retreat.

When Mbegu and her little herd of nine nursery orphans are ready for their next location, they are transported to the Voi Relocation Unit at Tsavo, to begin the next phase of their lives. When they arrive it's amazing, because the wild elephants and the orphans that have gone into the wild, all come to greet them. How do they know?

Mbegu settles into her new surroundings and carefully keeps her herd together to avoid any trouble. They have some special interactions with wild herds, and the wild herds love the orphans' new mudbath area. Now the fun begins with them slipping, sliding and sloshing around in the mud. One baby puts its trunk in the mud and happily blows mud bubbles. He doesn't want to leave!

Mbegu and her herd are braver and bolder now. They look forward to the wild interactions. This is the next step to joining a wild herd, having their own babies, and living their lives in the wild.

"I love watching the babies have a sloshy roll in the mud."

THE BIG MIGRATION

Every year thousands of animals migrate from the Serengeti to the Maasi Mara in search of fresh grass. It's a hazardous journey. Babies are born along the way, lions follow the herds to hunt and crocodiles lurk in the rivers to attack the animals as they make the dangerous river crossings.

After my many trips to Africa it is such a thrill to finally witness the big migration. I'm surrounded by millions of animals – zebras, wildebeest and antelope. I wish I had a tape recorder because the sounds of the animals all munching grass is amazing. Then I hear the deep grunting sound of the wildebeest and the shrill hee-haw of the zebras. No wonder they call it nature's greatest show on earth.

I wait for hours in the jeep and it's hot and dusty, then my guide tells me something is about to happen. The animals stop eating and start to follow their leader to the river. They stop. Thousands wait for the signal to cross. The big cats start to hunt, crocodiles wait, and the tension is terrible.

But, something spooks them. They all turn away from the river and start a dusty stampede back to the savanna. They will make the crossing another day. Meanwhile, the crocodiles slide into the water to wait.

Hyenas are scavengers. They follow lions to steal their food.

The wildebeest calves huddle together during the night to keep warm. A mother wakes up her own baby.

Thousands of zebras make the dangerous journey. Many calves are born along the way.

New cubs will be born during the migration because it's a successful time to hunt.

“Leopards are one of the most difficult animals to see in the wild because their camouflage is excellent.”

THE ELUSIVE

LEOPARD

Bahati with her kill hidden in the tree.

It is special to see Bahati's pregnant tummy as she walks towards me.

I ask my guide Nic about Bella 2, the blue-eyed leopard. He says Bahati, her mother, made a kill yesterday and it's well hidden in a tree. We go to explore. It takes time for me to see the kill wedged in the branches, but I can see Bahati, resting on a branch. I'm amazed the spindly branch can hold her weight because she's a large cat and is two months pregnant.

An hour later we circle back to see what she is doing. We hear the loud crunch of bones. Hyenas patiently wait under the tree for any scraps. We wait. And wait. And wait. Finally, she climbs down to a lower branch at lightning speed, has a rest, then continues to the ground. She walks past my jeep and I'm thrilled to be so close to her.

Then the day gets even better! Bella 2 starts to walk towards the tree that has her mother's kill. She stops close to the jeep and looks up at me. What a wonderful moment! It's a very special day because now I have fabulous photographs of three generations of beautiful leopards.

Leopards are nocturnal. They hunt during the night.

Leopards put their whiskers out when hunting and back when calm. Their whiskers are very sensitive and can feel the slightest vibration.

“See the necklace of ‘spots’ around the leopard’s neck? Each leopard can be identified by their unique circle of spots.”

When threatened, leopards will hiss, spit, growl, roar and make rasping yowls. But when happy, they make a loud purr.

Leopards are stealthy hunters and usually hunt at night. They're incredibly strong and carry their kill, which might be twice their body weight, high up into a tree. They can leap up to three metres and jump six metres. Wow, that's power! They feed on their kill for days, so I always look for a leopard's tail or legs hanging from a branch in a tree because that's their safe place to rest during the day.

Leopards drink water each day and surprisingly are great swimmers.

Nic says they are not dangerous animals and often hide from humans, so that's good to know. One night I heard an animal walking close to my tent, then I heard a coughing sound. I knew it was a leopard and I was safe.

Sadly, leopards are also endangered. They are killed for their fur and their bones are ground up for medicine. This is terrible – we don't need to kill one of the most beautiful animals in the world for a coat, a rug, or for any hope that it might cure a health problem.

SEEING

"I was so lucky to take this photograph of two perfect profiles."

DOUBLE

"I didn't realise zebras were endangered until I researched the Grévy and Mountain zebras."

It is a great challenge for me to get close to a herd of zebras because they're very skittish and gallop away as soon as I get close. As a result, I have many photographs of their decorative, striped bums. The zebras' stripes are a great camouflage when they herd together because the predator can't identify each animal.

The Burchell zebras live in large herds and once a year they migrate up to 800 kilometres in search of fresh grass on the Maasai Mara plains.

Zebras follow the dominant female in single file when they are travelling to a new grazing area.

The young calf's stripes help to camouflage it when it's among the herd.

A young foal drinking mum's rich milk. The fluffy tan stripes will turn black when it's older.

It's wonderful watching the young foal frolicking with its mum.

“Zebras look like a horse with stripes, but you can’t ride them. Their backs can’t carry a person’s weight.”

It's dangerous when zebras drink in the river because crocodiles can attack them.

Zebras like to roll in the dirt and this protects their skin from biting insects.

I like to follow herds of zebras on the grasslands to see all the different patterns on their decorative bodies.

I ask my guide how I can tell the difference between the Burchell and Grévy zebras. He says the Grévy zebras have big fluffy ears and their stripes don't go all around their stomachs.

The Burchell zebras have stripes all the way around their stomachs, and they have smaller ears. Grévy zebras are endangered with fewer than 2,500 left living in the wild.

The Grévy zebra with a different pattern of stripes.

The Grévy zebra's fluffy ears.

The fastest animal on land is the

CHEETAH

It's dramatic to witness a cheetah hunt. I watch as three male cheetahs focus on a tiny gazelle who is separated from the herd. My guide says they are too far away and a hunt would not succeed. But suddenly, one cheetah takes off like a bullet, reaching a speed of 100 kilometres an hour. It's incredible. He chases the running, zig-zagging gazelle and uses his tail like a rudder when he has to make a quick turn. I am so excited by the cheetah's speed and the fact that only one paw at a time touches the ground when he runs, that I forget to take a photograph. He catches the gazelle and his brothers join him to share the meal.

When a mother hunts for her cubs she will bring the bleating animal to them so they can practice their hunting skills. This is unpleasant to watch, but the cubs need to learn how to hunt and they must eat to survive. Cheetahs eat quickly and always look around for lions, hyenas, jackals or circling vultures, who want their share.

Cheetahs are diurnal meaning they are more active during the day.

"Cheetahs have incredible eyesight and can see up to five kilometres, but their night vision is very poor."

Cheetahs have over 2,000 black spots on their bodies. The black lines on their faces help to lessen the glare of the sun.

Three brothers, famous for being successful hunters, rest after the morning hunt.

When a cheetah starts to hunt it can accelerate up to 100 kilometres an hour in just three seconds.

A cheetah will scent-mark (having a pee) on a bush or tree to protect its home territory.

Cheetahs are devoted mothers, but their young cubs are always in danger.

The magic moment of my life.

Many years ago I was walking in the bush with a friend near Nanyuki, and I saw a cheetah strutting towards me. My friend told me to crouch down and be calm. I did and the cheetah came up to me. It was purring, so I wasn't frightened. I just thought it was the most amazing moment of my life. I put my arm out and the cheetah allowed me to stroke her.

I discovered that one cheetah had been rescued as an orphan and then released back into the wild. Because it was used to humans, it was not afraid of me, it was just curious.

The cheetah's fur feels the same as a dog's, but the fur on top of its head is coarse while under the jaw, the fur is so soft. Young cheetahs have a 'mantle', the fluffy fur that looks like a mane, and their purring sounds like a hundred cats.

On my recent trip my guide said cheetahs were jumping into jeeps using the height of the jeep to look for prey, but guides are being fined now if they allow this to happen. It's too dangerous.

See the difference between the cheetah and leopard spots.

Cheetah spots.

Leopard rosettes.

GIRAFFE

The Reticulated giraffe pattern.

PATTERNS

There are nine different patterns on the Nagolan, Kordofan, Nubian, South African, West African, Reticulated, Rothchild's, Thornicroft's and Maasai giraffes.

The Maasai giraffe pattern.

When my Encounter Mara guide, Francis, stops the jeep, I look up to see the tallest mammal on land; a beautiful giraffe. She stops to stare at me, then lumbers past the jeep. Then a mother walks past with her young calf, but it's skittish and tries to hide behind its mother. It looks at me with big brown eyes. It's adorable. Another young calf wobbles along on its spindly legs, I'm worried it's going to fall over, but the mother gently nudges it along.

I'm fascinated to see a giraffe give birth and I was surprised the mother gave birth standing up. The baby starts life by falling on its head, but is never hurt. My guide says a calf can run with its mother only ten hours after birth. If lions try to attack the calf, the mother will give the lion a lethal kick with her strong legs.

This is the first time I've seen so many giraffes in the wild, but it's time to go as we are making them nervous. We should never interfere with nature, so we drive back to camp.

It's dangerous for a giraffe to sit or bend down to drink. It makes it vulnerable as it can be attacked by a predator.

"The giraffe's neck has the same number of elongated vertebrae as humans. Isn't that amazing?"

"Giraffes usually fight by thumping their necks together, and this is unique. My guide calls it a kick-fight."

A giraffe twisting his long tongue around the thorns of the Acacia tree to eat the tender leaves.

I'm mesmerized. Just as the morning light turns a golden yellow, a journey of giraffes walks up to me. When they are close I see the oxpeckers (also called the tick-tick birds) pick insects from their manes and skin. When a giraffe opens its mouth, a bird pops inside to pick its teeth. Lucky giraffe – it has a mobile toothpick!

I've been coming to Africa for over 25 years and in that time I've only heard a giraffe make a noise, once. It was an odd sound, similar to a horse 'fluffing' with its lips. I also noticed the giraffe's mane vibrate up and down its neck, but I've never seen this strange action again.

Giraffes are gentle, beautiful animals. I love to get close to them at the giraffe sanctuary, just outside the city of Nairobi. They have a long sloppy 45cm blue-black tongue, and I get covered in spittle when I feed them. I don't care because it's a wonderful experience.

"Can you see the tiny dik-dik hiding in the branches?"

BEAUTY IN THE BUSH

"Gerenuks are the ballerinas of the bush, as they gracefully balance on their hooves to eat."

I was so lucky to see the elegant caracal hiding in the tall grass. It has long ear tufts that act as super-sound antennas.

There's a large rat-looking animal scurrying around my tent, and I'm not happy at all! But then I realise it's a mongoose and I follow it and discover its family. It is a delight to watch their antics and I'm surprised when they stand up like a meerkat. Mongoose have a reputation as ferocious snake fighters, so they will keep me safe. And they are safe too, as they are immune to snake venom.

The timid dik-diks are difficult to find in the bush. They have the unusual habit of going to the toilet in the same place. When I see a circle of poo pellets, I always know the dik-diks are nearby. I wait with my guide in the hope they will return.

To find the gerenuks, we search for trees that have been nibbled at the same height. Then we wait. It's a great reward watching them stand up to eat.

I've only seen the beautiful caracal once. Driving back to camp late in the afternoon, my guide spots the regal cat hiding in the grass. This is a special way to finish a day in the Mara.

The sweet little mongoose standing up like a meerkat.

There are many colourful lizards in Africa. This is the Mwanza agama.

Martial eagle.

Lilac-breasted roller.

Yellow-billed stork.

The martial eagle is a very powerful bird with a razor sharp beak and claws. It's been known to knock down a man. It has an enormous wing span of over two metres, so it's very dangerous. I always watch from a safe distance.

My guide has incredible eyesight and often stops the jeep to show me a tiny, exquisite bird. My African bird book is a must, so I can research along the way. I am fascinated to see the male and female ostrich perform a beautiful dance when they swing their feathered wings from side to side.

At night, owls make a soft, hooting sound, contrasting the roar of the lions. It's all part of the orchestra of sounds in the night.

The strutting secretary bird searching for insects.

Kingfisher.

Red-billed stork.

Fish eagle.

BIRDS

"From the flightless ostrich, the largest bird in the world, to the tiny kingfisher, there is a colourful variety of birds. What a thrill for bird lovers!"

DANGEROUS ANIMALS

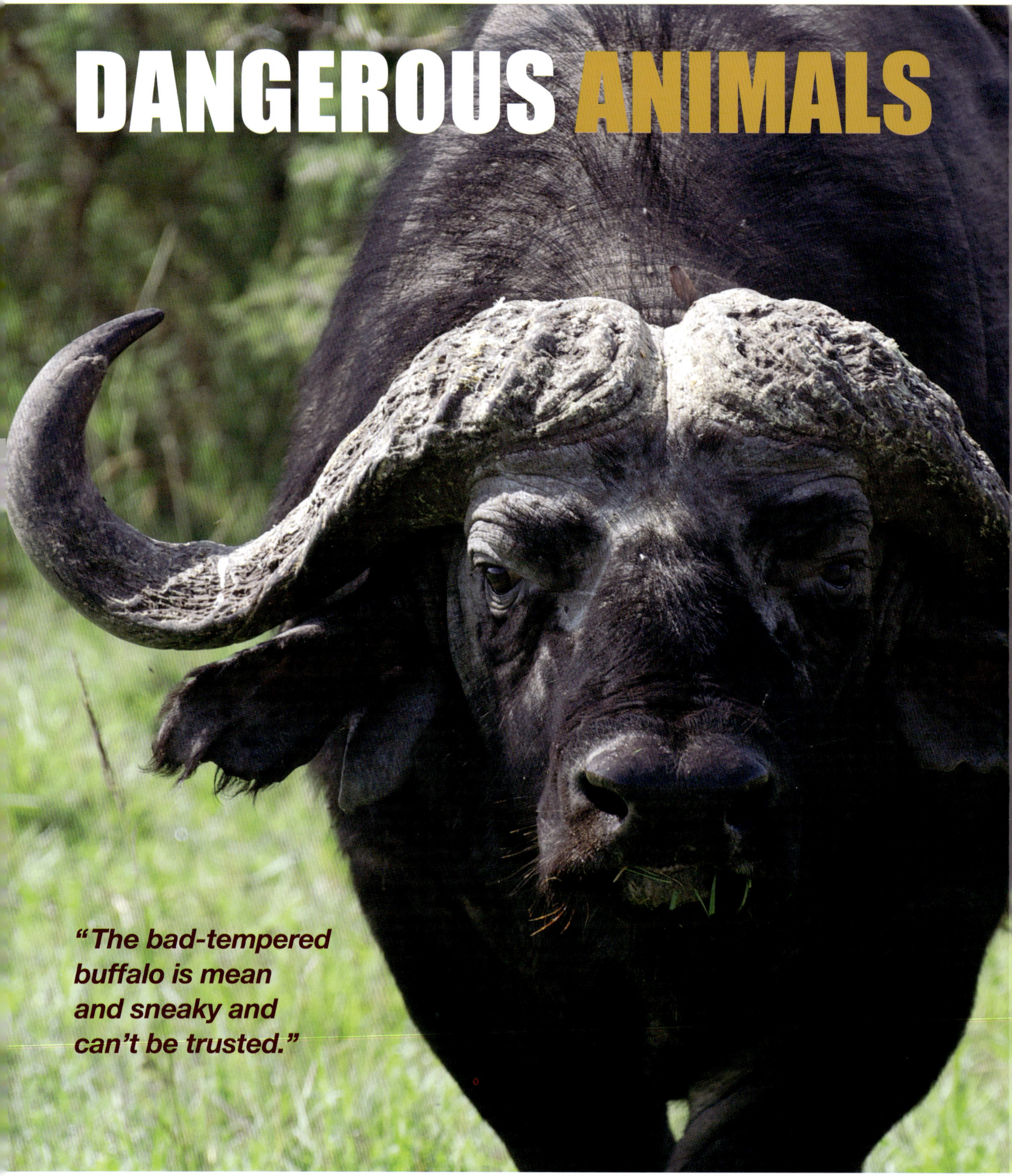

"The bad-tempered buffalo is mean and sneaky and can't be trusted."

"The hippo is the most dangerous animal in Africa."

I'm always frightened of hippos when they get close to me in the river. They can tip over the canoe and my guide has to paddle a quick escape. They live most of the day in the river, but in the afternoon, they will graze on grass next to the riverbank. If I get between them and the river they will attack me because they are fiercely territorial. This is the reason why more people are injured or killed by hippos than by any other animal, in Africa.

The rhino is also very dangerous. It has poor eyesight and will charge at anything that moves. Rhinos are also endangered because bad people kill them for their horns. They are ground up for Chinese medicine, a practice that should be stopped. Many species have disappeared from Earth never to be seen again, and humans are responsible for this disaster.

INTERESTING INFORMATION

"It's a thrill living in a tent in the Mara. I hear the throaty sounds of lions, the whooping of hyenas, and hippos munching grass outside my tent."

I've been to Africa 11 times, and I've had good and bad experiences with camps. I book my Asilia camps with **Troy Smith** now, because he created special safaris for me when I was writing my series of **True to Life Books**. He's worked in the bush in both Kenya and South Africa and enjoys exploring new regions. *Troy@trueafrica.com*.

Troy with Ringo the rhino.

I enjoy the **Asilia Africa** camps and have returned many times. The accommodation includes eco-friendly tented camps in wildlife-rich reserves in Kenya and Tanzania. ***https://www.asiliaafrica.com/***

My tent at Encounter Mara camp.

My tent at Rekero camp.

The family tent at Nabiosho camp.

The Maasai men are wonderful with children.

I met **Dr Tammie Matson** when she organised a special tour in South Africa for a film crew. I had just started creating animal videos for my **True to Life Books**, so this was a great opportunity to tag along and learn.

Dr Tammie Matson is a zoologist and wild-life conservationist with a special passion for elephants. Through her company she runs specialist tours to Africa to connect people to wild places and wildlife. As a mother of two young children, Tammie has a special interest in sharing Africa with families.
https://www.matsonridley.com/
https://www.matsonridley.com/blog

When I travel to Nairobi, I always stay at **Macushla House**. It's a comfortable ranch-style house with beautifully-appointed rooms, a pool and great service. The staff are wonderful and book reliable taxis to drive me to the giraffe centre, and to the elephant orphanage. ***www.macushla.biz macushla@africaonline.co.ke***

At the **Giraffe Centre** you can climb onto a tall platform and come face-to-face with a beautiful giraffe to feed it. That is a very special experience!

The **Sheldrick Elephant Orphanage** is about half an hour in a taxi from Macushla House and the driver can wait for you. I've visited their orphanage many times and I never tire of watching the young elephants and their funny antics. They greedily suck on their milk bottles while the head keeper gives an interesting talk. Then comes the fun! It is hilarious watching the babies enjoying their mud bath.

WOULD YOU LIKE TO ADOPT AN ELEPHANT?

You can help to save an orphaned elephant by fostering on the Sheldrick Wildlife Trust website. You will receive a special certificate, a beautiful watercolour painting by Angela Sheldrick and a monthly update about how your baby is surviving.

I've adopted nine baby elephants over many years and it has been a wonderful and rewarding experience. My first adoption was Yatta, and now she is living with a wild herd and she has two calves of her own, called Yetu and Yoyo. A great success story that I'm proud to be part of.

www.sheldrickwildlifetrust.org

It's always good to know a few polite Swahili words when you visit Africa.

Jumbo – hello and have a good day
Hakuna matata – don't worry, not a problem
Asante sana – many thanks

ANIMAL NAMES

Baboon - *Nyani*
Buffalo - *Nyati / Mbogo*
Cheetah - *Duma*
Crocodile - *Mamba*
Dikdik – *Digidigi*
Eland - *Pofu*
Elephant - *Tembo / Ndovu*
Gazelle - *Swala*
Giraffe - *Twiga*
Grant's Gazelle - *Swala Granti*
Guinea fowl - *Kanga*
Hippo - *Kiboko*
Hyena - *Fisi*
Impala - *Swala pala*
Jackal - *Mbweha*
Leopard - *Chui*
Lion – *Simba*
Monkey – *Tumbili*
Oryx – *Choroa*
Ostrich – *Mbuni*
Rhinoceros - *Kifaru*
Thompson's Gazelle - *Swala tomi*
Topi - *Nyamera*
Vervet Monkey - *Tumbili / Tumbiri*
Warthog - *Ngiri*
Waterbuck - *Kuro*
Wildebeest - *Nyumbu*
Zebra - *Pundamilia*

Author and photographer, Jan Latta, has been creating books for children so they can learn about endangered animals. For over 25 years she has travelled to Sri Lanka, Borneo, Uganda, India, China, Costa Rica and eleven times to Africa. See her free educational videos of animals in the wild on ***www.truetolifebooks.com.au***